WHY DO YOU SPEAK AS YOU DO?

WHY DO YOU SPEAK AS YOU DO?

A Guide to World Languages

Kay Cooper

Illustrations by Brandon Kruse

Walker and Company
New York

Author's Note: In languages that don't use roman alphabets, words are
spelled out in roman letters.

First published in the United States of America in 1992
by Walker Publishing Company, Inc.

Published simultaneously in Canada by Thomas Allen & Son
Canada, Limited, Markham, Ontario

Library of Congress Cataloging-in-Publication Data
Cooper, Kay.
Why do you speak as you do? :
a guide to world languages / Kay Cooper.
p. cm.
Summary: Discusses the phenomenon of language, how it may have
developed and how it is learned, and gives an overview of such
languages as French, Japanese, and Hebrew.
ISBN 0-8027-8164-0.—ISBN 0-8027-8165-9
1. Language and languages—Juvenile literature. [1. Language and
languages.] I. Title.
P106.C595   1993
400—dc20   92-15632
CIP
AC

Printed in the United States of America

2 4 6 8 10 9 7 5 3 1

For John J. Watt, Jr.

Contents

Acknowledgments

The author acknowledges the kind assistance of the following people: Chin Kim, coordinator of Asian, Pacific, and Other Languages Office, Los Angeles Unified School District; Gaylene Amorasak, Thai interpreter, Springfield, Illinois; Paul Schmidt, Latin instructor, Bloomington, Illinois; Danaë Thompson, Arabic interpreter, Park Forest, Illinois; Ann Watt, French student, Alexandria, Virginia; Kathryn Zable, Spanish instructor, Batavia, Illinois; Sister Leanne Hanselman, Japanese interpreter, Springfield, Illinois; Usha Arshanapally, student, India; Rita Organ, associate curator of African American materials, The Children's Museum of Indianapolis; Jie Xia, student, Beijing, People's Republic of China; and Marianne Stowers, German interpreter, Springfield, Illinois.

WHY DO YOU
SPEAK
AS YOU DO?

★ 1 ★

WHAT IS LANGUAGE?

As you read this sentence, quietly say, "Itchy, knee, san, she, go." Now laugh (ha-ha) and say, "Ohio."

In the first sentence, you counted to five. Then you said, "Mother," and finally you greeted someone in the morning. And you said it all in Japanese!

In all these sentences, you used your voice, tongue, lips, and teeth to make certain sounds. These sounds have certain meanings. You know and understand what these sounds mean in English. And a Japanese knows and understands what they mean in Japanese.

When you speak a language—regardless of which language it is—you use sounds to match your thoughts, ideas, and feelings. The trick is to find the

1

right sounds in your language to express what you want to say. People who know your language understand what you are saying. That is what language is all about. It's a system of vocal sounds you use to communicate to people.

When you hear people talking in a language you don't understand, you probably think they're talking gobbledygook. Such strange noises are coming out of their mouths that you can't believe they actually are talking. Not only are they making sounds you've never heard but they're running all their sounds together. You have no idea which sounds begin a word and which ones end a word. Their sounds make about as much sense as the noises of croaking frogs.

If you've never heard a strange language, imagine that you are a puppy trying to follow your master's commands. The only problem is that your master doesn't speak dog. He speaks Bariai, a language spoken on the island of New Britain in Papua New Guinea, which is north of Australia. Your only hope is to wait for a hand signal that might communicate to you what he wants you to do. Meanwhile, you watch your master intently while listening to a weird *bada* sound.

Since you're smarter than the dog, you might think that *bada* means "bad dog." That's a good idea, but *bada* really means "to fetch."

Imagine buying a dictionary in this language and looking up words so you could say to the dog's master something like "Hello! Nice dog there." Then the master might understand you. But if he says something to you, you won't understand it or be able to look up his sentences in the dictionary.

You also will use the sounds in your language to pronounce the words in his language. And he'll do the same. You'll not understand each other because many of the sounds in your language are not sounds in his language. Each language has its own set of sounds, which make up the words of that language.

Imagine making all the sounds you can possibly think of—*ayki, kler, nappe, z-z-z-z, eka eka*. No language contains all the sounds you can make. For example, Thai and Japanese don't have the *v* sound of the English word *vat*. The *th* sound in English is not a sound in French, Japanese, or Thai. So if you speak French, you probably pronounce *this* and *that* as if they were spelled *zis* and *zat*. English doesn't have the *ich* sound that occurs in the German words *ich* and *dich* ("I" and "you") or the *ach* sound in the German words *auch* and *acht* ("also" and "eight"). And the sound you make when you sneeze is not a part of any word in any language.

Some of the sounds you make are hard for you to use as parts of words. For example, clicking noises you make with your tongue and kissing noises are sounds in a language spoken in southern Africa. Speakers of this language have no problem using these sounds as parts of words. Just for fun, substitute a click for part of your name. For example, Katie could be *Ka click* or *Click t*. Say your new-sounding name to a friend. Does your friend understand you? How hard is it for you to use a click for every time you make a *k* sound and a kissing sound for every time you make a *p* or *b* sound?

It's amazing how all the sounds that people can make ever became words in the first place. No one knows how language started, but there are several ideas. Perhaps the first word sounded something like "goody-hoo," which imitates the sound an owl makes. "Goody-hoo," spelled *gwdihŵ*, is the Welsh word for "owl." The idea that language started when people began to identify animals by their sounds is called the *bow-wow theory*. This idea isn't hard to imagine. When you were two years old, you probably called a dog *bow-wow*, a duck *quack-quack*, and a sheep *baa-baa*.

Or, perhaps the first word uttered was *ow!*, which still is *ow* or *ai* in most languages today. If *ow* were one of the first words, then language began as an expression of pain, dislike, or hunger. The idea that language began in this way is called the *pooh-pooh theory*.

Another idea, called the *ding-dong theory*, suggests that people first made up words to imitate the noises they heard, such as *boom* for thunder and *splash* for water.

Then again, perhaps language didn't start until people began working together. Prehistoric people who lived in caves had to work together to drag home large game animals that they'd killed. They also rolled immense rocks to block off cave entrances from roaming beasts. While doing these tasks, they may have sung simple songs. This idea, called the *yo-he-ho theory*, may explain how songs and poetry began. You

4

can remember this theory by connecting it with the song sung by the Wicked Witch's guards in the movie *The Wizard of Oz*.

Even though no one knows how language began, scientists think that the first words were spoken by people who lived in Africa some 200,000 years ago. From the language that these people spoke came all the world's languages.

The idea that all languages were once the same language is found in the story of the Tower of Babel in the book of Genesis in the Bible. According to this story, people spoke only one language until they began building a gigantic tower that would reach to heaven. The project was so ambitious that God thought if people could build the tower they could accomplish anything and, therefore, they would not serve him. So God stopped the building by changing the language of the people so that they couldn't understand one another and work together.

A similar story is told in Mexico, where the great pyramid of Choulula was built to provide a refuge from a future flood. Again the language of the people changed.

Linguists, people who study languages, think that languages began to change when the people who spoke the first language migrated out of Africa to other lands, such as India and Europe. These people never returned to their homeland, and, in time, their language changed.

From that prehistoric language came *Proto-Indo-European*. *Proto* comes from the Greek word meaning "first," and *Indo-European* comes from the geographic area where the language was spoken.

Linguists piece together Proto-Indo-European and other prehistoric languages by looking for clues hidden in words. They compare words spoken in all languages as well as ancient words written on clay tablets. By studying all these words, linguists find similar sound patterns, similar structures in grammar, and common-sounding words. They analyze how these words have changed over thousands and thousands of years and then go beyond these years to reconstruct words no one has ever seen written or heard spoken. In this way, linguists piece together prehistoric languages much as you would put together a puzzle—piece by piece.

Linguists are especially interested in words that everyone uses, such as words for natural objects (moon, sun, water) and words for body parts (eye, ear, arm). They think that the original word for "water" was *haku*, which tens of thousands of years later became *hakw* in Proto-Indo-European and thousands of years after that became *wazzar* in Old German. When words in ancient languages are reconstructed, they give clues to what the speakers of these languages saw and ate, and how they migrated to new lands.

According to recent work by two Russian linguists, reconstructed words in Proto-Indo-European suggest that the people speaking this language were farmers. Since many of their words had to do with mountains and rivers, they probably lived in a hilly area some 8,000 years ago.

By combining word clues with archaeological

6

clues dug up from the ground, linguists think that these ancient farmers originally lived in an area known as Anatolia, which is now central Turkey. From there they migrated across Europe and into India and Russia to set up farms. As they moved, they took their language with them.

Words in many other languages, such as Latin, Russian, and English, are thought to come from Proto-Indo-European. These languages have many similar words. For example, the English word *mother* is *mater* in Latin, *madre* in Spanish, *Mutter* in German, and *mat* in Russian.

Latin was the language of the Romans who invaded an island in the Atlantic Ocean during the first century. They named the island Britannia after the natives, who called themselves Britons. The Britons spoke a Celtic language, which also comes from Proto-Indo-European.

For 400 years Celtic and Latin were spoken on Britannia. Then tribes from present-day Germany, the Netherlands, and Denmark crossed the North Sea and invaded Britannia. The invaders settled on the island, bringing with them a language that later would be known as English.

★ 2 ★

WHAT IS ENGLISH?

Do you understand *hund, dēor, stān?* These are Old English words for "dog," "animal," and "stone." Frisians, who live today in the northern part of the Netherlands and western Germany, understand these words. They speak a Western Germanic language and live in the area that was once home to the Germanic tribes who crossed the sea to Britannia.

The Frisians along with other Germanic tribes, such as the Jutes, Saxons, and Angles, settled in different parts of Britannia in the fifth century and brought their own languages with them. No one knows how well these tribes understood one another, but one group—the Saxons—eventually overpowered the others. Their language, which was a West Saxon variety of the Germanic language, gradually became English, and their country became England.

The Saxons believed in many gods. The main ones were Tiw, Woden, and Thor. The names of the days Tuesday, Wednesday, and Thursday come from the names of these gods. Friday is named for Woden's wife, Frig. Sunday and Monday come from the Old English words for sun and moon.

Old English is very different from modern English. For example, "The man slew the king" can be written in Old English as "Sloh se man pone kyning," or "Sloh pone kyning se man." Translated, these sentences are "Slew the man the king" and "Slew the king the man." Both are grammatically correct in Old English, because word order didn't matter very much. What mattered was the endings added to words, because the endings gave a sentence its meaning. *Se* was used only with subject nouns, and *pone* was used only with object nouns.

Most Old English words didn't survive to become modern-day words. Yet over 4,000 were passed down to us. They are the words we most often use: *child, sister, brother, man, wife, eat, sleep, house, speak, write, word*. The prepositions (*but, in, on, at, for, to, of*) are Old English words too.

Do you recognize *scip, boeo,* and *bricg*? These words changed in spelling but not in pronunciation. We still say *ship, bath,* and *bridge*. The pronunciation for these Old English words isn't hard to learn. For example, *i* is our *ee* sound and *e* sounds like *ay*.

Three hundred years after the Germanic tribes invaded Britain, the Saxons faced attacks from Viking sea warriors from Denmark and Scandinavia. These

10

attacks continued until 878, when a treaty was signed that gave the Danes from Denmark control of the northeastern part of the island and the Saxons control of the southwestern section. Today this division reflects the areas where the northern and southern varieties of British English are spoken.

For a long time, the Danes spoke Old Norse, another language from Proto-Indo-European, while the Saxons spoke Old English. The languages had similar vocabularies, so speakers of Old Norse and Old English could understand each other.

Years passed, with the Anglo-Saxons and Danes living peacefully. Then, in 1066, the French invaded and killed Harold, king of England. The French invaders were Normans, the descendants of Vikings who had settled along the northwestern shore of France, known as Normandy. On Christmas Day 1066, William I, duke of Normandy, became king of England.

The life of the French king and the people he brought to England is echoed today in the English language. For example, farm animals are called by their English names (*sheep, cow,* and *pig*), but, once their meat is brought to the table, they are given French names (*mutton* from *mouton, beef* from *boeuf,* and *pork* from *porc*). These words give you clues to the way the Saxons and Normans lived. The Saxons raised and slaughtered the animals, while the Normans cooked and ate the meat. Most English words that describe food preparation—*boiled, roast, fry, pastry, soup, jelly,* and *sauce*—have come into English from Old French.

The French also brought scholars and craftsmen to England. Thus we have the English words *artist* from the French *artiste, tailor* from *tailleur, rhyme* from *rime,* and *poem* from *poème.*

But what happened to Old English? It survived as the language spoken by the Saxon peasants and tradespeople. One of these people was Robin Hood, who robbed from the rich Normans to give to the poor Saxons. Imagine that you somehow traveled 630 years back in time to talk to Robin Hood. Do you think you'd understand him? Would he have said the "veather ist cold"?

The English that Robin Hood used, called Middle English, is much closer to modern English than it is to Old English. A language resembling Middle English is spoken today in the German state of Schleswig-Holstein, which borders southern Denmark. This area, called Angeln, was once home to the Angles, one of the Germanic tribes that invaded Britannia. These people came from the *angle* or the corner of the land. From the Angles came the word *England,* which comes from *Angle-land,* meaning "Land of the Angles." In Old English, the Angles were called *Engles,* and their language was known as *englisc.*

People who spoke Middle English pronounced certain sounds that we no longer hear. The biggest difference was in the way they pronounced vowels. For example, the word *hous* (house) rhymed with *moose,* and *home* rhymed with *gloom.*

It wasn't until the time of the great English poet Geoffrey Chaucer (1340–1400) that people began to pronounce their vowels more as we do today. Linguists call this change in pronunciation the Great Vowel Shift. The only problem was that English spelling didn't keep up with the change. Many English words still are spelled the way they were before the shift took place. That's why English is such a difficult language to spell. Just look at the spelling for one vowel sound in *bloom, who, blue, blew, fruit, soup,* and *plume.* Middle English speakers didn't pronounce these vowels alike, but we do.

Normans began speaking more English when they started thinking of themselves as more English than French. Cut off from France by the English Channel, the Normans married English women and raised their children to speak French and English. They also spoke a variety of French known only in England. Their harsh, crackling talk contrasted so much with the soft, smooth Parisian French that Parisians began to make fun of the way Normans talked. Rather than be insulted for sounding inferior and uneducated, the Normans began to speak more and more English. Eventually, English became the language of the land; in 1399 England had a king—Henry IV—who spoke English.

The English that survived, however, was a very different language from the Old English spoken by the Germanic tribes. In fact, everything about the language—spelling, vocabulary, pronunciation, and grammar—had changed.

The histories of other languages show similar changes; most languages develop slowly through time. One language that has not changed much is Icelandic, which is similar to Old Norse, the language of the Vikings. Icelanders can read and understand Old Norse words written 1,000 years ago.

Think how wonderful it is that languages change slowly. If languages changed quickly, you probably would have to relearn English every ten years or so.

★ 3 ★

YAWL CALL THAT TAWK AN ACT-CENT?

Do you know why your friends recognize your voice over the telephone? It's because no one talks as you do. No one says the same sounds exactly the way you do. And, *you* have an *accent*. People hear your accent when you pronounce *bomb, calm, cart, caught, cot, good, horse, house, oil,* and *water.* A special computer program can tell you where you live depending on how you pronounce these ten words.

But you don't have to say these words to reveal where your home is.

Do you go to *skOOuuhl*? You call western Texas home.

Do you have birthday *potties*? You're either a New Englander or live in New York State east of the Hudson River.

15

Do you like ice cream *combs*? Your home is in the South.

Do you eat all your *vegetibbles*? You live in North Carolina.

Do you call those twinkling lights in the night sky *stores*? You live in southern Utah.

If your native language is Spanish, you probably are told that you have a Spanish accent when you speak English. You probably were born in a Spanish-speaking country.

You can discover a lot about accents by listening carefully to the pronunciations of people who are interviewed by news anchors on the major TV networks. Listen to the New England fisherman, western cowboy, southern mayor, and Texan rancher. By listening carefully to the way these people pronounce their words, you can get a good idea of how different American accents are.

If you call up your friend on the telephone one rainy morning and say, "Ids a litill drippin a-outside so mutter's gwine carry us dis moanin," you have more than an accent. You're speaking a *dialect*. A dialect includes the way you pronounce words as well as your grammar and vocabulary. In this Southern dialect, you are telling your friend that it is raining outside so Mother is going to take us (in the car to school) this morning.

The three main dialect groups of the United States are General American, Southern, and New England. *General American* is spoken in New York State west of the Hudson River, New Jersey, Delaware, Pennsylvania, and all of the Midwest, North

Central, Rocky Mountain, and West Coast states. The *New England dialect* is spoken in all six New England states and in New York State east of the Hudson River. The area covered by the *Southern dialect* includes all states, except Delaware and West Virginia, which are south of Pennsylvania and the Ohio River, and east of an imaginary line running from St. Louis to the middle of the Rio Grande River and down that river to the Gulf of Mexico. These main dialect groups can be traced to the people who first settled North America.

The Pilgrims who sailed to Massachusetts in 1620 were from the old Anglian communities of Norfolk, Suffolk, and Essex, where the *a* in *bath* was pronounced like the *a* in *bard*. You still can hear the Pilgrims' broad *a* accent today in New England when people say *dahnce, cah-nt,* and *bah-th* (dance, can't, bath).

Settlers who arrived later from this same area in southern England dropped their *r*'s before consonants and at the ends of words. These people settled in New England and along the Atlantic seacoast.

Later, settlers came from northern England, where the Saxon tribes had lived. These people kept the *r* in their words and settled farther inland, away from the Atlantic.

Tracing the history of the *r*-less and *r* groups reveals how early American settlers migrated. Those who kept the *r* tended to move westward across the American frontier, thereby breaking contact with Britain and the Americans living along the Atlantic coast. Those who spoke the *r*-less dialect didn't migrate as much and kept contact with Britain and the changes

17

occurring in British English. This migration partly explains why the English used in large sections of the Midwest and West is similar. In fact, some linguists estimate that today almost two-thirds of Americans speak with the same accent.

If you listen very carefully to the way people talk, you can hear the influences of America's early settlers in their speech. You hear the dropped *r* when a New Yorker tells you that he or she lives in "New Yoahk" and then says words such as *gull, hot,* and *bey-eh* (girl, heart, bear). If you've never heard a New Yoaker, listen to Bugs Bunny. He has a New York accent mixed in with a little Brooklyn and Bronx.

You also can hear the dropped *r* along with the broad *a* sound when someone with a *Hahvahd* (Harvard) accent says, "Pahk the cah in Hahvahd Yahd and wawk ta da hahbuh" (Park the car in Harvard Yard and walk to the harbor).

Don't think that all the people in one dialect group talk the same way. They don't. The main dialect groups can be broken down into numerous smaller dialect groups. In New England, for example, the people of *Bahston* (Boston) shift the vowel sound *au* to *ah*, while on *Cape Caud* (Cape Cod) the *ah* sound is *au*. Cape Codders also drop their *r*'s but add another syllable. They pronounce *there* as *they-uh*, while Bostonians say *theah*.

You also can hear influences of the Southern dialect in parts of New England where people make a *y* sound after the letters *d, n,* and *t*. The result is heard in words such as *dyu* and *nyu* (due and new).

The Southern dialect began as a type of speech

18

coming from the southern part of England, where the *r* was dropped and where people often spoke with a whine. (If you don't know what a whine is, listen to the voice of a Siamese cat.) The way the "proper" British spoke also greatly influenced the Southern dialect because southerners in the eighteenth century were involved in commercial trade with Britain. Southern speech also was influenced by the speech of African slaves, who were used to work the plantation fields.

You can pick out a Southern accent because southerners pronounce their words very slowly, drawling out certain vowel sounds. The result is words such as *ti-ahm, po, fi-ahn, I-ah,* and *tyune* (time, poor, fine, I, and tune).

In addition to English settlers, other immigrants came to different regions of America. Each group influenced the language of the areas in which they settled. You still hear influences of the German language when someone—perhaps even you—stresses words like *IN-surance* and *JU-ly*.

You also can hear an English dialect known as Pennsylvania Dutch, especially in Lancaster County in southeastern Pennsylvania. This dialect is a descendant of Rhine Frankish, a German dialect spoken along the Rhine River in Germany. The Pennsylvania Dutch are Amish, a religious group originally from Switzerland who settled in Pennsylvania in 1683. Perhaps the dialect's best-known expression is "Outen the light" for "Put out the light."

The most recent groups of immigrants to the United States have come from the Asian countries of

Thailand and Vietnam, and from Spanish-speaking places such as Mexico, Puerto Rico, Cuba, and the Dominican Republic. Each group has influenced and enriched the regional dialects of the communities in which it has settled.

If you live in a Mexican community in Los Angeles, you probably speak a dialect known as Chicano English. This is a variety of the English language spoken in major urban areas of the United States. Chicano English, however, is different from the dialects spoken by Puerto Rican and Cuban immigrants living in Miami, Florida. Differences are found in accents, special expressions, and word choices, just as differences are found in the Spanish spoken in Madrid, Spain, and Mexico City, Mexico. An *autobús* (bus) in Spain may be called a *guagua* in the Caribbean.

When Spanish-speaking immigrants first come to the United States, they see many new items, learn the words for these objects, and then mix Spanish and English to say something like "Tengo tennis shoes" (I have tennis shoes).

Spanish speakers usually substitute the Spanish vowel system for the English so that many words sound alike. *Ship* and *sheep*, for example, are both pronounced *sheep* because *i* in Spanish is pronounced like the *e* in *seek*. Spanish speakers also substitute *ch* for *sh* (*che* for *she*) because *sh* is not a sound in their language, but *ch* is.

If you live in Los Angeles, you probably hear young people speaking a variety of English known as African American English. What's strange about this is that their parents speak Chinese or Vietnamese.

These young people speak African American English because it is the English spoken by their friends in school and in their neighborhoods, where they have learned English. They often use more than one negative word in a sentence (I don't never go there) and leave out the verb *to be* in their sentences (She nice).

Some speakers of this English don't pronounce the *r* between vowels, so that *Carol* is pronounced *Cal*. Other speakers are *l*-less, so that *help* is pronounced *hep*.

African American English resembles a dialect spoken in the South before the Civil War. Africans kept in slavery who spoke different languages were grouped together so they couldn't communicate. The white plantation owners feared that otherwise they would plan revolts. Thus slaves learned English as it was used by whites to communicate with them. This language was a simple trade language or *pidgin*, containing between 700 and 1,500 English words mixed in with some African words.

A pidgin is similar to a language you would speak if you suddenly were taken to someplace like Nepal in the Himalaya Mountains of Asia, where people speaking Nepali would tell you what to do. In order to get along in your new situation, you would use all that you know about language to try to communicate a few simple words.

Pidgin languages were spoken on slave plantations in the South, on the islands in the Caribbean Sea, and in Hawaii. In time, these languages developed into more complicated languages called *creoles*.

Slaves born on plantations considered these creoles to be their native languages.

If you had been the child of a southern plantation owner in pre–Civil War days, you probably would have been raised by a black woman and would have played with black children. Thus, you would have picked up many features of their talk in your speech. Later in your life, you might have been sent to school in England, where you would have acquired a British accent.

One example of an English-based pidgin is found in the speech of characters in the Uncle Remus stories written by Joel Chandler Harris. In these stories, Uncle Remus, a former black slave, tells the young son of his employer a series of African fables, which include tales about Brer Rabbit, Brer Fox, and Brer Wolf. These characters speak *Gullah*, which still is spoken by the descendants of West African slaves on the islands off the coasts of Georgia and South Carolina. Several African words, such as *yam* and *okra*, have passed into the English language through Gullah.

If you live in the Ozarks in Missouri or in the hills of the Appalachian Mountains in the eastern United States, you may pronounce words in a way similar to the way the great English poet and playwright William Shakespeare did. People living outside your area probably think you use "hillbilly" words— *yourn* (for *yours*), *hisn* (for *his*), and many others. Even though your area was settled many years after Shakespeare died, your hill community was isolated from the language changes occurring in other regions of the country. Thus, language in the hills didn't change as much as it did in other areas, and, therefore, many old expressions and pronunciations are still used. Perhaps instead of *ate* you say *et*, which is the British past form of *eat* used by the early settlers along the Atlantic coast.

If you live in Louisiana, you may speak a language called *Cajun*, which is a mixture of French, English, Spanish, German, American Indian, and African American expressions. Cajuns are descendants of French Canadians who were expelled by the British from Nova Scotia in 1755. Moving to southern Louisiana, they continued to speak French. But their French vocabulary didn't have words for many of the new things and ideas they encountered, so the Cajuns developed their own language. Cajun terms include *rat du bois* (rat of the woods) for opossum and *sac a lait* (bag of milk) for a type of fish.

So be careful when you talk. The way you pronounce words and the expressions you use tell more about you than you think.

★ 4 ★

How Do You Know How to Talk?

What was the first word you said? And how old were you when you said it? If you don't know, ask your parents. Perhaps they have a baby book in which they wrote down your first word and when you said it.

If you compared the time you said your first word with the times first words were said by people born in places such as China, Norway, and Egypt, you would discover that everyone said his or her first word at age four to six months. Everyone made the same babbling baby sounds about the same time too. No matter where you were born and live, you learned to talk in much the way everyone else did. That's because you are programmed to learn language, much the way a computer is programmed to run a certain software

25

package. When you were a child, one language was not harder or easier for you to learn. In fact, you easily could have learned two very different languages by the time you were five.

As a baby, you made sounds that occur in all languages. You made German vowel sounds, the French guttural *r*, and many other language sounds. When you talk now, you only make the sounds you were encouraged to repeat because they are sounds in your language. The other sounds you were making, in languages such as Korean and Arabic, disappeared because no one encouraged you to repeat them.

Sometime after your first birthday, you realized that the sound *shoe* was somehow associated with an object you wore on your foot. Your parents probably repeated *shoe* and pointed to a shoe countless times before you finally got the idea and said "shoe."

At age two, you put two words together, like "Toy mine" and "Daddy here." Half a year later, you came up with utterances such as "Joel want that" and "Me put toys back." Because your language was so simple in structure, it was similar to a creole.

At age five, you added about twenty words per day to your vocabulary and came up with sentences such as "The water fountain is playing peekaboo" and "Where does it say on my report card that I'm real cute?" At age six, you knew about 8,000 words. While you were learning words, you also were learning grammar rules. No one taught you these rules, you just picked them up by hearing people talk.

If you now are over age twelve and are trying to learn another language, you probably are having difficulty. No one knows why this is true, but to realize that a three-year-old learns a language much more easily than a college student does is frustrating. To help you along, here are some facts you should know before learning a new language:

1. Letters. Many languages use updated versions of the roman alphabet, which is the alphabet English uses. But familiar-looking alphabet letters in other languages do *not* always sound like English letters. In German and Polish, the letter *w* is pronounced *v*. And in German the letter *v* is pronounced *f*. In Spanish, *j* is pronounced *h*, and *ll* is pronounced *y*. *Ll* is considered one letter in Spanish, even though it is made up of two characters. If you're learning a language that uses a different alphabet, such as Russian, Thai, and Arabic, then you don't have to learn new ways to pronounce familiar-looking letters.

2. Spelling. Do you have problems with spelling? You're not alone. Anyone studying English will tell you that English spelling rules are among the most difficult to learn because they are so illogical and inconsistent. As you know from reading this book, English spelling rules were established hundreds of years ago, so words are spelled today the way they were pronounced centuries ago. Spanish, German, and Turkish have simple spelling rules. French is a little harder.

3. Pronunciation. Remember when you were a child and imitated the sounds of airplanes,

galloping horses, and fire engines? You listened very carefully to these sounds and then imitated what you heard. When you learn a new language, you'll have to listen very carefully to sounds again and then imitate strange noises such as *rrrr-rrrr*, *ffffvvvv*, and *chchchrr*. Don't feel embarrassed when you make these sounds. You're learning a new way to talk.

When you learn another way to talk, you also learn a new way to hear sounds. People who speak other languages hear certain sounds differently than you do. Dogs don't "bow-wow" in France, for example. The French hear them "oua-oua." Dogs "bu-bu" in Italy and "wan-wan" in Japan.

Spanish and Italian are the easiest languages for you to learn to pronounce because they don't have many sounds that are much different from those in English. All the Spanish vowels have different sounds, but, once you learn them, you're well on your way to mastering Spanish because it is written almost exactly as it sounds. Spanish has only two silent letters—*h* and sometimes *u*. The only silent letter in Italian is *h*.

French and German are harder to pronounce. Some sounds in these languages seem almost like English sounds, but if you listen carefully you'll realize that they are very different. Arabic is among the hardest languages to pronounce because it has sounds that are rarely found in other languages. And Chinese and Japanese words don't seem to have the separate and distinct sounds of English.

Many languages use accents or other special marks over and under letters. These marks are often clues to the way words are pronounced. French has a mark called a *cédille*, which occurs beneath a *c*, as in the word *français*. A cedilla means that the letter *c* is pronounced *s*. Other marks you'll see in this book are accent marks (` ´) and a mark called a *tréma* (¨), which is two dots placed over some vowels.

Most world languages have *tones*, or musical pitches, that help distinguish one word from another. Thai, for example, has five tones. The Thai word *naa* can mean "nickname," "rice paddy," "young maternal uncle or aunt," "face," or "thick" depending on the tone (low, mid, high, falling, and rising). Tone marks above Thai's alphabet of characters tell which tone is to be used. A *2* with a comma or a vertical dash above a character are some of the tone marks used in Thai. If you don't have a good ear for tones, you'll have problems distinguishing words in tone languages, such as Chinese, Burmese, and many American Indian languages.

4. Vocabulary. English has the largest vocabulary of any language in the world because it has adopted tens of thousands of words from more than fifty languages. As a result, it is the only

language that needs books of synonyms like *Roget's Thesaurus*. A *synonym* is a word that is close in meaning to another word. For example, some synonyms for *talk* are *dialogue*, *conversation*, and *speech*. Of the millions of English words, about 200,000 are commonly used. This is more than German (184,000) or French (100,000).

Once you begin learning a new language, you'll find the following techniques helpful:

1. Connect new sounds with objects. When you hear a meaningless sound, immediately picture in your mind what that sound means. When you hear the sound *eye* in English, you think right away of two round objects that allow you to see. So when you hear the sound *ojo* in Spanish, you can immediately think, "That sound means the two round objects that allow me to see." Match a sound with a mental picture or an idea of an action over and over again in your mind. After a while, the meaningless sound will produce the correct picture in your mind.

   If you can't think of an easy way to remember certain words, invent something. Put the words you have trouble remembering into funny sentences. Find a friend who is studying the same language and practice talking with that person.

2. Play a word game with your new words. When you play the word game Scrabble, you use letters to make a word. Sometimes you can

make another word by adding certain letters before and after the original word. These additions are called *prefixes* and *suffixes*. You add them to basic word roots to change the meanings of words. For example, you add *de* and *pre* to the Latin word root *scribe* to get *describe* and *prescribe*.

Once you learn the basic word roots of the language you're studying, you will be able to build more and more new words. In Russian, for example, the word root *pisat'* means "to write." By adding the prefixes *o* (about) and *vy* (out), you get the words *opisat'* (to describe) and *vypisat'* (to prescribe).

3. Create new sentences. Each language has its own way of putting words together to express ideas. You use a certain word order in English by placing the subject first, the verb second, and the object last. People who speak other languages might not use the same word order. The song title "Throw Mama from the Train a Kiss" uses a word order found in languages such as German and Polish.

Sometimes languages are classified according to the basic word order they use. There are six orders: SVO (subject, verb, object), SOV, VSO, VOS, OVS, and OSV. French and Thai are two languages that have the same word order as English.

4. Use a tape recorder. Listen to language tapes and recordings, and use a tape recorder to record yourself speaking a new language. By

practicing with a tape recorder, you will become familiar with the new sounds you're making.

5. Have fun! Choose a new name in the language you're studying. Join a language club, speak with exchange students in your area, and seek out a pen pal who speaks your new language by writing to the International Friendship League, 55 Mount Vernon Street, Boston, Massachusetts 02108, or to World Pen Pals, 1690 Como Avenue, St. Paul, Minnesota 55108.

Don't be afraid to make mistakes. Everyone does. Your mistakes will help you learn how your new language works.

★ 5 ★

CAN YOU CLIMB A LANGUAGE FAMILY TREE?

Speaking one language is much like living in an enormous palace and staying in only one room. You can't go to the other rooms because all the doors are locked with special language keys. Each key represents a different language, and you must speak that language before you can turn the key and unlock the door. Thus, if you learn another language, you can enter a second room. If you learn a third language, you can live in three rooms, and so on. Living in these rooms is exciting because they are full of new and fascinating people, ideas, and cultures.

Perhaps you already are learning a second or third language in school. Some second-graders in public schools in Virginia, Oregon, and Alaska are learning Japanese. They think that learning Japanese is fun because they can surprise their parents with a language they don't know. Young people attending kindergarten through sixth grade in Los Angeles public schools are learning Spanish, and some will be learning Korean. Sixty to 80 percent of the instruction in these classes is conducted in a second language. In other schools across the country, teachers switch from English to Spanish and back again.

If your native language is English, the easiest languages for you to learn belong to the same language family as English. The hardest ones are not related to English. What does this mean?

The history of all the world's languages can be drawn out as a large family tree, much as you would draw a tree of your own family showing how you are related to your parents, grandparents, and great-grandparents. Thus, languages can be classified like people according to whether they are Smiths, Browns, or Johnsons.

One gigantic branch on the language family tree is the Proto-Indo-European family, which is divided into several groups or small branches. About half the people in the world speak a language belonging to Proto-Indo-European.

The *Germanic* language branch divides into two main groups, Western and Northern Germanic. Western Germanic languages include English, German, Frisian, Dutch, Flemish, and Yiddish. Northern Germanic languages include the Scandinavian languages—Icelandic, Danish, Swedish, and Norwegian. All the Germanic languages are related because at one time they were the same language.

The Germanic language is the "parent" language to all the languages in the Western and Northern groups, which are called its daughters. Thus, English is a sister to German, and Danish is a sister to Swedish.

Another branch of languages coming from Proto-Indo-European includes the *Romance* languages—Spanish, French, Rumanian, Italian, and Portuguese, as well as Provençal (spoken in southern France) and Catalan (spoken in northern Spain). The Romance languages are daughters of Vulgar (meaning "common") Latin, which was spoken throughout the Roman Empire over 2,000 years ago. This is not the Latin you may one day study in high school or college. That is Classical Latin, which is the written or literary form of Latin. The language of the Roman Catholic Church is Ecclesiastical Latin, which resembles Vulgar more than Classical Latin.

Latin started to change into the Romance languages when the Roman Empire began to collapse around the year 200. Because Latin speakers were separated from one another by mountains and long distances, they developed their own Latin dialects. In time, these dialects developed into separate languages, which we call the Romance (meaning "Roman") languages. The Romance languages have many words that are similar. For example, the word *nose* is *nariz* in Spanish and Portuguese, *naso* in Italian, *nez* in French, and *nas* in Rumanian.

On the language family tree, the five Romance languages are cousins to English. This means that at one time Latin and Germanic were sisters. This also means that there are many relationships between English and the Romance languages. One relationship is found in the letters *f* and *p*. Whereas an English word begins with *f*, the corresponding word in a Romance language often begins with *p*. The word *father* is the French *père* and the Spanish *padre*. *Fish* is the French *poisson* and the Spanish *pescado*.

German

About half the words in English come from the Germanic language. They are words that you use every day. See if you can guess the meanings of these German words: *Mutter, Vater, Bruder, dumm, Bibel* (mother, father, brother, dumb, Bible). Look-alike words that have the same or similar meanings in two or more languages are called *cognates*. But watch out for false cognates—look-alike words that have different meanings. For example, *Gift* in German means "poison," not "a present." *Fussball* is the most popular sport in Germany, but it's not football. It's soccer.

As in English, German words can be grouped into categories. Knowing the word *Zimmer* (room) helps you to figure out the meanings of other words in the same category: *Badezimmer, Zimmerpflanze, im Nebenzimmer* (bathroom, houseplant, in the next room).

Did you notice that all the nouns in the previous paragraph are capitalized? That's because in German all nouns are capitalized. And many of them are very long. When Germans need new words, they don't create them. Instead they string nouns together, as in *Volksschullehrer*, which means "elementary school

38

teacher." The first part of this word, *Volk*, means "common people," *Schul* means "school," and *Lehrer* means "teacher."

When Germans talk about a person, place, or thing, they don't say something like "cat, dog, and rat." They say, "the cat, the dog, and the rat." And they use different words for *the* as well as different forms for the words *a* and *an*. *The, a,* and *an,* which are called *articles*, often tell to which class or *gender* a noun belongs. For example, *der Junge* (the boy) belongs to a class called masculine, *die Note* (the grade) to a class called feminine, and *das Mädchen* (the girl) to a class called neuter. "Girl" is neuter because all nouns with the ending *-chen* are neuter. English is one language that does not have different forms and rules for the articles *the, a,* and *an*.

What words do you use when you give a report in front of the class? When you talk with your friends? Your parents? Grandparents? Adults on the telephone? The speech you use in different situations is called your *speech style*. English does not have strict rules that govern style. Unlike English, many other languages use different forms of words to reflect the social situation the speaker is in. The German *du*, which (as well as the French *tu*) means "you," is used with a person the speaker knows well, such as a family member or a close friend. A more formal word (*sie* in German and *vous* in French) is used with a person the speaker doesn't know well or with an older person.

Look at this list and cover up the words in the right-hand column. How many German words can you identify just by guessing?

German Word	English Word
Banana	banana
Fotoapparat	camera
Fuss	foot
Garten	garden
helfen	to help
Hund	dog
lernen	to learn
Mathematikbuch	math book
Milch	milk
Morgen	morning
Schule	school
singen	to sing
Sommer	summer
Strasse	street

Did you notice in this list that the German *ss* comes out in English as *t*? This is one relationship between German and English words. Keep your eyes open for such relationships. They will make the learning of a new language easier. Did you also notice that German infinitives (verbs used with *to*) always end in *-en* or *-n*?

Spanish

You also know or can guess the meanings of many Spanish words. Spanish and English share many cognates because they are language neighbors, and have borrowed words from each other. Thus, the English term *roast beef* has become the Spanish *rosbif*, and the Spanish *el lagarto* (the lizard) has become *alligator*.

The similarities between Spanish and English words will help you learn Spanish. Cover up the words in the right-hand column in the following list and see how many Spanish words you can guess.

Spanish Word	English Word
avión	airplane
calculadora	calculator
decidir	to decide
escuela	school
estudiar	to study
familia	family
nada	nothing
oportunidad	opportunity
realidad	reality
refrigerador	refrigerator
sándwich	sandwich
sol	sun
tarde	tardy

How many language relationships did you find in the list?

You probably noticed that where a Spanish verb ends in -ar, -er, or -ir, the corresponding English word is an infinitive (to decide, to study). You also may have noticed that where a Spanish word ends in -dad, the corresponding English word ends in -ity.

If you study another Romance language, you'll discover that many words beginning with h in Spanish begin with f in the other Romance languages. For example, the Spanish word for "son" is hijo, and in French it is fils. When you learn Spanish, you'll be able to read Portuguese, although you'll have problems understanding what a Portuguese is saying.

Italian

Once you learn Spanish, you should have little trouble learning Italian, which many linguists think is the most beautiful language in the world. Of all the Romance languages, Italian is the closest to the original Latin. Its dialects differ greatly, however, so that Italians who speak different dialects have problems communicating.

Cover up the words in the right-hand column of the following list. How many of the following Italian words you can guess?

Italian Word	English Word
artista	artist
città	city
colore	color
dottore	doctor
emozione	emotion
famiglia	family
gloria	glory
identità	identity
penna	pen
qualità	quality
rosa	rose
scuola	school
sincero	sincere
sole	sun
stazione	station

How many language relationships did you notice? Where an Italian word ends in *-zione*, the corresponding English word ends *-tion*. Where Italian words end with *-a* or *-ia*, the corresponding English word ends with *-y*. Italian words that are spelled like English words have a vowel sound (*a*, *e*, or *o*) added at the end. Did you also notice that all the words in this list end in vowels? Few Italian words end in consonants.

French

You already know thousands of French words. Many are cognates: *train, chocolat, particulier, Husky sibérien, gouvernement, oncle, bleu, carotte, adorer, zéro*.

In the following list are French words that are related to English words. Cover up the words in the right-hand column and see how many French words you can identify by guessing.

French Word	English Word
famille	family
grand-père	grandfather
lampe	lamp
liberté	liberty
lion	lion
nom	name
occuper	to occupy
parfum	perfume
plume	pen
professeur	professor
regarder	to look at
riche	rich
soleil	sun
sports	sports, games

43

Did you notice that some of these words are similar to words in the Spanish and Italian lists, since words in all these languages come from Latin? These words are: *familia-famiglia-famille* and *sol-sole-soleil*.

As you see in this list, most infinitives in French end in -er (occuper, regarder).

Second Cousins

When you look at words that are *not* from the Germanic or Romance families, you will discover that it becomes harder to find language relationships. That's why languages outside the Germanic and Romance families are harder for you to learn.

The *Celtic* languages, for instance, include Irish, Scots Gaelic, Welsh, and Breton. Celtic speakers live in Ireland, Scotland, and Wales, the northwest coastal region of France, called Brittany. The *Baltic* languages—Lithuanian and Latvian—are related to English. Of all the Proto-Indo-European languages, Lithuanian has changed the least. In fact, Lithuanians can understand simple Sanskrit, which is the ancient language of India. Languages that are distant cousins to English include the *Iranian* languages (which include Persian), the only *Hellenic* language (which is Greek), and the eleven *Slavic* languages (which include Russian, Polish, Czech, and Bulgarian).

Russian

The Russian alphabet was invented in the ninth century by two Greek missionaries, Saints Cyril and Methodius. Calling their new alphabet *Cyrillic* after Saint Cyril, they based it on the Greek alphabet, borrowed a couple of Hebrew letters, and made up the rest.

44

The Russian alphabet has thirty-three letters. Of these letters, *a*, *k*, *m*, *o*, and *t* have approximately the same sounds as in English. The letter *b* sounds like *v*, *h* makes an *n* sound, *p* sounds like *r*, *c* makes an *s* sound, *y* is an *oo* sound, *x* sounds like *h*, and *e* is pronounced *eh* or *yeh*.

Russian nouns are masculine, feminine, or neuter, and all change their endings according to how they are used in a sentence. For example, *-a* is used on many subject nouns and *-u* is used on many object nouns, as in the word *sobaka* (dog), which becomes *sobaku* when it is the object of a sentence. Russian also classifies all its past tense verbs into masculine or feminine and its adjectives into as many as sixteen forms. In English, only one adjective has had two forms—*blonde* and *blond*. (*Blonde* for a female, *blond* for a male.) *Blond* is now the preferable spelling when referring to either sex. Words for the articles *the*, *an*, and *a* do not exist in Russian.

Russian has many long words, such as *dostoprimechatelnosti*, which means "sights." Names of people and places can be very long.

A few Russian words have been adopted into English, such as *sputnik*, *tundra*, and *czar*.

Hindi and Urdu

Hindi is a daughter of Sanskrit, the ancient language of India. Thus, Sanskrit is a distant cousin to Latin and Greek. Hindi is very much like Urdu, which originally was a Hindi dialect, spoken for centuries in the area around Delhi, which is in north India. But Hindi uses Sanskrit characters for its alphabet, which is called *Devanagari*, and Urdu uses an Arabic script.

Hindi is written from left to right, while Urdu is written from right to left. Most Hindi words come from Sanskrit, while Urdu has borrowed many Persian and Arabic words.

Hindi is one of the main languages of India. Urdu is the main language of Pakistan and also is spoken in India.

In Hindi, you don't call your brothers and sisters by their names. Instead, you call an older sister *didi*, an older brother *bade bhaiya*, a younger sister *choti behen*, and a younger brother *chote bhaiya*. If you must distinguish between more than one sibling, you use the person's name before these words, such as *Usha didi* (sister Usha) or *Ravi bhaiya*. (brother Ravi). As you may have guessed, *didi* means "elder sister," *behen* means "sister," *bhaiya* means "brother," *choti* means "small," and *bade* means "elder."

Hindi has fun-to-learn *echo words*, which are rhyming words used to express similarities, such as *roti voti* (bread and baked goods) and *khana peena sona* (eating drinking sleeping). For emphasis, Hindi repeats words as in *dheere-dheere* (slow slow), which means "very slowly."

English words of Hindi origin include *cot* and *loot*.

Greek

Greek, one of the oldest Proto-Indo-European languages, is spoken in Greece and on the island of Cyprus in the northeast Mediterranean Sea. There are two forms of modern-day Greek: *demotic* for everyday conversation, and a written language, known as *pure*, which is closer to the ancient Greek than demotic.

46

Both the spoken and written languages use the same sounds, but there are differences in vocabulary, sentence structure, and grammar. An older form of Greek, called *Koine*, is used today by the Eastern Orthodox Church. Koine was the language of the people from the time of Alexander the Great some 2,300 years ago to the middle of the sixth century.

Modern Greek uses the ancient Greek alphabet. This writing system, adopted by the ancient Greeks over 3,000 years ago, came from the Phoenicians and had twenty-two signs. The Greeks changed the system because the Phoenicians had more consonants in their language than the Greeks did. The Greeks used some of the Phoenician consonants to represent their vowel sounds and then added certain letters for more vowel sounds. Thus, each sound in Greek had its own sign. This alphabet was the first in which letters stood for vowels as well as for consonants. It was used by the pre-Latin people of Italy, the Etruscans, who passed it on to the Romans. The Romans spread it all over the world. Many modern-day languages, including English, use updated versions of the roman alphabet.

When the Romans conquered Greece over 2,000 years ago, a large number of Greek words were adopted into the Latin language. Thus, many Greek words came into English through Latin. From the Greek word *demos* (common people) and the suffix *-kratia* (power), we get *democracy*.

Some Greek prefixes and their meanings are *amphi-* (around, about, and both), *arch-* (chief and prime), *hemi-* (half), *pro-* (before), and *pseudo-* (false). Some Greek suffixes and their meanings are *-meter* (measure), *-graph* (write), and *-scope* (see).

47

★6★

MEET YOUR DISTANT RELATIVES

If you live in a large city, such as Boston, Chicago, or Los Angeles, you'll hear many languages being spoken. A walk through the hallways of any Los Angeles public school, for example, will bring you to people who speak Chinese, Spanish, Armenian, Japanese, Korean, Russian, Filipino, and Farsi (an Iranian language). More than eighty-three languages are spoken by students throughout the Los Angeles Unified Public School District, which offers high school instruction in eight.

Some of these languages are not related to English and, therefore, are difficult for English speakers to learn. However, they're not as difficult as *Basque*, which is perhaps the hardest language of all. Basque was spoken by cave people living in Europe over 2 million years ago. Called Euskara by its speakers, Basque is still spoken by people who live around the Bay of Biscay in Spain and France. Basque's words and the way the language is put together are so difficult that, according to an old Spanish proverb, "When God wished to punish the Devil he condemned him for seven years to study Basque."

If you learn one language not related to English, it's easier to learn a second language in that language group. For example, Arabic and Hebrew are *Semitic* languages and closely related. If you learn one of these languages, it's easy to learn the other because of the similarities between the two. You can even tackle *Aramaic*, the language that Jesus probably used, since it was the everyday language spoken 2,000 years ago in Palestine. Aramaic is spoken today in parts of Lebanon, Turkey, and Iran.

Hebrew and Arabic

The main language spoken today in Israel is Hebrew, which is based on Biblical Hebrew, the language in which the Old Testament was written. Thus, young Israelis can read and understand manuscripts written in Hebrew 2,000 years ago. Although Hebrew has some harsh guttural and sharp hissing sounds, it sounds very musical when spoken.

Hebrew and Arabic can be written using only consonants because vowels are understood as a person reads along. Vowels can be indicated by marks, such as small dots or dashes, placed above and below letters. These marks are used in elementary school textbooks and in some religious books. They are left out of other writings, so that the reader must figure out word meanings by using *context clues*. For example, Arabic has many *homographs*, words that are spelled alike but are pronounced differently, as in the English *lead* (to guide or direct) and *lead* (a lead pencil). When you read *lead* in a sentence, you know its meaning by seeing context clues, or the words surrounding it. (For fun, try writing a sentence in English using only consonants; then ask other people to figure out what you have written.)

Both Hebrew and Arabic are written from right to left and from the top of the page to the bottom. The Hebrew alphabet contains twenty-two letters, while the Arabic alphabet has twenty-eight. Most Arabic letters have four forms, depending on whether the letter stands alone, comes at the beginning of a word, is written between other letters, or is used to end a word. The different forms that letters take make Arabic a hard language to learn—even if you speak Hebrew.

Arabic has more deep guttural sounds than any other language. Its consonant sounds, which are spoken with great emphasis, influence the pronunciation of the surrounding vowels.

Arabic word roots consist of three consonants. If you want to change the meaning of the word root, all you do is add vowels. For example, the Arabic root that conveys the general meaning of writing is *ktb*. Vowels are added to indicate specific meanings. Thus, *katib* means "one who writes," *kitab* means "book," and *uktub* is a command word, "write!"

Spoken Arabic varies from country to country,

51

but classical Arabic has remained largely unchanged since the seventh century. Classical Arabic is the language of the Koran, the sacred book of the Islamic religion.

Written Arabic is understood by anyone speaking the language because all Arab countries use the same writing system, called *Puristic Arabic*. Derived from the writing of the Koran, Puristic Arabic has a very formal style and does not include slang words and expressions.

Arabic has contributed numerous words to English, many of them beginning with *al-*. These include *algebra, alfalfa,* and *albatross*. English words of Hebrew origin include *rabbi, sabbath,* and *amen*.

Chinese

The language family with the most speakers is *Sino-Tibetan*, which includes Chinese, Thai, and other languages of Southeast Asian countries.

Chinese has thousands of dialects, some of which are so different that people from different areas don't understand each other. But all Chinese people use the same writing system, *kanji*. Kanji doesn't use sounds to represent objects and ideas. Instead, it uses characters. For example, the character for "mouth" is a square (口) and three mouths together (品) mean "criticism" or "criticize." If you draw vapor coming out of the mouth (言), you've written "word" or "speak," but if you draw a solid object coming out of the mouth (舌), you've written "tongue." By the time a Chinese child is ten, he or she has learned about 200 characters. But one needs to learn about 4,800 more to read a newspaper. Chinese dictionaries contain from 40,000 to 50,000 characters.

The main dialect, spoken in northern China, is called *Mandarin*. The Chinese call it *putonghua*, which means "standard language." Dialects differ in the use of tones, or musical pitches, used to distinguish one word from another. Mandarin has four tones—high, rising, low, and falling. Other dialects have as many as nine tones. The Mandarin tone system is much like the rising tone for questions and the falling tone for statements spoken in English.

Most Chinese words are one syllable, and tenses (past, present, future) do not exist. Chinese has unisex pronouns—*he*, *she*, and *it* are all *ta*. Opposites are put together to express what they describe. For example, in Chinese *big-small* means "size," *long-short* means "length," and *sell-buy* means "business."

Chinese is like Italian in that few of its words end in consonants. The most common consonant endings are *-n* and *-ng*. Chinese grammar rules are simple and easy to learn.

English words of Chinese origin include *tea*, *typhoon*, and *shanghai*.

Japanese

Do you take piano lessons? If you do, you probably have a metronome that ticks off a steady beat so you can play the notes to a certain rhythm. Imagine yourself speaking each syllable, or word part, of every word you say to the click of the metronome. Such a steady and even way of speaking mimics the way a Japanese talks.

53

But you don't have to say many words in Japanese to complete a sentence. You only need a verb. If you want to add more meaning, you can add a noun in front of the verb. You also can change the meaning of the sentence by adding different tones to the verb. And you can change the meaning by adding other parts of speech, such as adjectives and prepositions. Whatever you do, keep your verb at the end of the sentence.

All Japanese words end in either vowels or the consonant *n*. Consonants that sound much like English sounds are *b*, *ch*, *f*, *g*, *h*, *j*, *k*, *s*, *sh*, and *w*. Japanese doesn't have words for the articles *the*, *an*, and *a*; there isn't any difference between singular and plural (dog/dogs), and the future tense (shall/will) doesn't exist.

Japanese dialects can be divided into three groups, according to differences in tone and accent pattern. Standard Japanese is spoken by most of the people. The second dialect is are called *Kansai*, or Western, and then there's a single-pattern type.

Japanese is spoken in four styles—intimate, polite, honorific, and impersonal. The Japanese distinguish between levels of politeness by the verb they use. A Japanese eating in a restaurant uses one verb form to speak to the waiter, another to a dinner guest, another to a family member, and so on. Swear words do not exist in Japanese.

If you listen to a Japanese man talk, you'll hear snapping sounds. You'll hear soft sounds when a Japanese woman speaks. This is because men and women use different dialects. These two dialects are so different that guide dogs are trained in English because their owners' sex is unknown during the training, and it would be most embarrassing for the dog's new owner to have to use the "wrong sex" dialect.

Japanese usually is written in columns from top to bottom beginning on the right side of a page. Words in some books, however, are written across the page so that English words can be included.

English words of Japanese origin include *karate* and *hibachi*.

Vietnamese and Korean

Spoken throughout Europe and Asia are languages that do not seem to be related to any family group. They include Japanese, Vietnamese, and Korean.

Vietnamese is a tone language like Thai, which sounds very musical when spoken. The same word spoken in six different tones or pitches has different meanings. It is as if in English the word *dog* spoken in a singing tone of F flat would be "golden retriever" and in C sharp would be "mountain." Nearly half of the words in Vietnamese come from Chinese, and many are one syllable long.

Vietnamese has three main dialects—northern, central, and southern. They are about as different as American dialects. Since the seventeenth century, Vietnamese has been written in a roman script called *quoc-ngu*, which means "national language."

If you hear someone speak Korean, you'll hear rigid sounds that are spoken in a rhythm similar to that of Japanese. The style of Korean also resembles Japanese because it changes as Koreans speak to different people. Koreans show respect or the lack of it by changing the endings of the verbs they use. Korean, like Vietnamese, has borrowed many Chinese words. Korean has six main dialects, which most Koreans can understand. The Korean alphabet, called *Han'gŭl*, has twenty-four symbols. It was invented by King Sejong, the Korean ruler from 1419 to 1450. The writing is different from that of most other languages because the letters of each syllable are written together in clusters, as if the English word "language" were written

LA　　GU
N　　AG
E

North Korea uses only Han'gŭl, while South Korea uses Han'gŭl and some Chinese characters.

American Indian Languages

Languages spoken by native American Indians belong to the *Amerindian* family. Unfortunately, many of these languages are spoken by only a few older people. When a language is no longer spoken, it is called a *dead language*. It "dies" because there are no children to learn it.

Today, many Amerindian languages as well as almost half of the world's languages are in danger of disappearing. Some of these languages are being preserved because native speakers are using microcomputers to write about their cultures. One such language is Nähnü (NYAW-hnyu), the native language of thousands of Indians in Mexico. It is preserved because Jesús Salinas Pedraza, a schoolteacher in the Mexican state of Hidalgo, wrote about his culture in Nähnü, using a version of an alphabet developed by missionaries. Until Pedraza's work, Nähnü was an unwritten language.

Indian languages spoken north of Mexico were not written until 1821. At that time, a Cherokee silversmith named Sequoyah (seh-KWOH-yuh) produced eighty-six written characters to represent every sound in the Cherokee language. These syllable signs, which Sequoyah spent twelve years creating, were so simple and logical that they could be learned in a few days. Thus, thousands of Cherokees quickly learned to read and write.

Today the most widely spoken American Indian language in South America is Quechua (pronounced KECH-ua), which is spoken by some 6 million people living in the Andes Mountains of Peru, Bolivia, and Ecuador.

The largest American Indian language groups in North America today are the Algonquian (which includes Cheyenne and Blackfoot, spoken mainly in Montana, and Cree, spoken principally in Ontario, Canada) and the Athapaskan (which includes Navajo, spoken principally in Arizona, and Apache, spoken mainly in Oklahoma).

Scholars think that Indians first came to America some 25,000 years ago from Asia, crossing the small land bridge that spanned the Bering Strait between present-day Alaska and Russia. Although these people were all hunters, they differed from one another in language, customs, and physical appearance. Over the centuries, their descendants migrated southward until they eventually inhabited the southernmost tip of South America.

By the time Europeans began settling America, the land was populated with many cultures of Indians, ranging from hunting tribes to the civilizations of the Inca, Aztec, and Maya.

English words of Indian origin include chipmunk, raccoon, coyote, woodchuck, barbecue, canoe, and potato.

About half of the fifty states in our country take their names from an American Indian language. *Minnesota* means "sky blue waters" in Sioux, and *Oklahoma* means "red people" in Choctaw. Many American cities have Indian names, such as Tallahassee (old town), Chattanooga (rock rising to a point), and Chicago (the place of the skunk cabbage).

Esperanto

Of the 3,000 languages spoken today, one is made up and is spoken by about 8 million people in 110 countries. This language, called Esperanto, was invented in 1887 by Ludovic Zamenhof, an eye doctor who lived in Poland. Zamenhof dedicated himself to universal tolerance, which he hoped to promote mainly through the development of an international language. Esperanto has sixteen basic rules, which never change. For example, words are pronounced as they are spelled, all nouns end in -*o*, with plural -*oj*, and all adjectives end in -*a*, with plural -*aj*. The present tense of a verb ends in -*as*, the past tense in -*is*, and the future in -*os*. The alphabet has twenty-eight letters. Esperanto is not difficult to learn. You can master it in one year if you study the language three hours per week.

If you are interested in learning Esperanto, you can enroll in a free postal course by sending a stamped, self-addressed envelope to Esperanto Express-S, 410 Darrel Road, Hillsborough, California 94010.

What Is an Official Language?

An official language is the language in which the government of a country conducts its business. English is the official language of forty-four countries, including the United States. But, by the year 2000, more people in the United States will speak Spanish than English. This is because increasing numbers of Spanish-speaking people have emigrated to Texas, Florida, California, and New York from Spanish-speaking countries near the United States. Do you think that someday the United States will have two official languages—English and Spanish?

Almost one-fourth of the world's countries have two official languages, and some have even more. Kenya, which is on the eastern coast of Africa, uses English and Swahili. *Swahili*, originally a creole, has adopted several English words, such as *jipi* (jeep) and *parashuti* (parachute).

India, which has 1,652 languages, uses fifteen official languages, with Hindi as its first. Once ruled by England, India uses English as one of its official languages. India's constitution was written in English, and about 5 percent of the people speak English. No language is spoken by more than 16 percent of the population.

The official language in most South American countries is Spanish, but more people speak Portuguese. The Portuguese speakers are in Brazil, which covers nearly half of the continent.

Your New Language

When you begin learning a new language, you'll want to know more about the cultures of the countries whose language you are studying. You'll want to know what these people are like, what they do every day, and what is important to them. Knowing this information will help you if you ever visit or work in a country where your new language is spoken.

If your new language is spoken by people in your neighborhood or school, you soon will be able to talk to these people in their language and make new friends. By speaking two languages, not only can you prepare yourself to live in a global world but you can serve as a bridge between the United States and those countries where your new language is spoken.

If you want to learn a language that is not taught in your school, ask your teacher or school librarian to help you find a language program or a language teacher. *Viel Glück!*

Glossary

Accent—the way you pronounce words or the emphasis placed on a certain syllable of a word.

Alphabet—the set of letters, characters, or signs used in writing a language. The word *alphabet* comes from the first two letters of the Greek alphabet, *alpha* and *beta*.

Cognates—words in different languages that look alike and have the same or similar meanings.

Creole—a former pidgin that has acquired native speakers. Creoles are rarely written. *See* Pidgin.

Dead Language—a language that is no longer spoken.

Dialect—a variety of a language usually spoken by certain groups of people in certain areas of a country. Most languages can be broken down into dialects. These dialects are different in pronunciation, grammar, and vocabulary.

Gender—a system in many languages in which all nouns fall into one class or another. For example, German has three classes of nouns, called masculine, feminine, and neuter.

Language Family—a group of languages that are related to one another because they all have developed from a single ancestral language.

Linguist—a scholar who studies languages scientifically. Linguists usually speak several languages.

Pidgin—a simple language spoken in addition to one's native language. When a pidgin becomes the native language of a group of people, it is called a creole. *See* Creole.

Speech Style—Speech used in different social situations.

Index